Finally, a book on American politics that every American can understand and agree with. Corruption exists and thrives in both political parties and continues regardless of who has the majority. Both the red and the blue are equally dirty and that includes all three branches; executive, legislative, and judicial, and all with equal contempt for the intelligence of the American people.

C is for Corruption provides a beautifully illustrated, bitingly humorous presentation of our country's broken political system and the inept leadership that ensures it stays that way. Liars, thieves, killers, and sexual predators (otherwise known as our normal government) are all included.

Copyright © 2021 by Alan J. Yeck
All rights reserved. No part of this book may be reproduced or used in any manner without written permission of the copyright owner except for the use of quotations in a book review.
ISBN 978-1-7371324-8-6 (paperback) ISBN 978-1-7371324-9-3 (ebook)
Published by Happy Hippies Media, LLC

is for ABSCAM. This was the name of an undercover FBI operation in the late 1970s that resulted in one senator, six congressmen, and more than a dozen other corrupt officials being arrested and convicted of accepting bribes.

B is for BILL CLINTON. He was the 42nd President of the United States and only the 2nd in the history of the country to be impeached. He lied under oath about having an affair with a 21-year-old Whitehouse intern. Bill has had many women claim he molested them. Other words for Bill Clinton include, cheater, liar, and sleazebag.

C

is for CORRUPTION. It means the abuse of power or position for personal gain. There are many forms of corruption, including bribery, embezzlement, and extortion; our Congress knows them all well. Other words include, graft, crookedness, racket, kickbacks, embezzlement, and profiteering.

D is for DEMAGOGUE. This is a "leader" whose passionate rhetoric promotes greed, fear, and hatred, often through lying. Other words for demagogue include fanatic, inflamer, inciter, instigator, and politician.

6

E is for EXTORTION. It's when a person uses power and threats, to get money or to do anything else the extortionist wants done. Politicians extort other politicians and/or have been extorted by corporations and criminals for something they're trying to cover up.

F

is for FRAUD. It is another way of lying that hurts the people victimized from it. This could be someone elected in Congress that takes tax dollars and uses them for their own purposes. Our current student loan system is an example of fraud involving lots of people and institutions.

G is for GERRYMANDERING, where corrupt politicians manipulate voting district boundaries. Both Republicans and Democrats change the area of who can vote for them and this helps them win, or hurts the other party. Other words for gerrymandering including cheating, manipulating, fixing, doctoring, and cracking and packing.

is for the HATCH ACT. The Hatch Act of 1939 is a United States federal law that was enacted because corrupt politicians were using intimidation or bribery of voters, and federal employees to campaign for them.

I

is for IRAN-CONTRA. The Iran-Contra Affair was a political scandal during President Ronald Reagan's Administration. Weapons were secretly sold to the Islamic Republic of Iran (against the law). They took the money from the illegal sale and gave it to the Contras in Nicaragua (against the law). Eleven people were convicted but all were pardoned when Reagan's Vice President, George H. W. Bush, became president.

J

Is for JUDICIAL SYSTEM, in the U.S. is the system of courts that administer justice and constitute the judicial branch of government. Many federal, state, and local judges have been bought with bribes to influence their decisions.

K is for KLEPTOCRACY. This is when corrupt leaders (kleptocrats) secretly, enrich themselves through kickbacks, special favors, bribes, or misappropriation of government monies to themselves and friends.

L is for LOBBYISTS. Lobbyists are hired, and paid by corporations and special-interest groups to influence elected officials to vote for the way it benefits their clients. Lobbyists spend lots and lots and lots of money on politicians for this. Politicians listen to lobbyist much more than they do the people who voted for them.

M is for MONEY LAUNDERING. This is taking ill-gotten gains from criminal activity and disguising its illegal origins. It is widely practiced by drug traffickers, corrupt politicians, corporations, and human traffickers. Bank secrecy laws make laundered money particularly hard to trace. Hmmm, who makes those laws? Oh yeh, the same corrupt politicians who benefit from them.

N is for NEPOTISM. A form of favoritism where a person exploits their power and authority to the benefit of unqualified people by giving them a job or go government contract. Many politicians at all levels have used this for family members or to pay back some form of debt.

O is for **OFFSHORE BANK ACCOUNTS**. This is where politicians, corporations, banks, and drug dealers try and hide their money in non-U.S. institutions like the Cayman Islands. Besides concealing illegal activity, they can also avoid paying any U.S. taxes.

P is for the Pentagon Papers. This was a classified history of the political and military involvement of the U.S. in Vietnam from 1945 to 1967. The papers exposed that four different presidential administrations (Harry S. Truman, Dwight D. Eisenhower, John F. Kennedy, and Lyndon B. Johnson) had lied to justify the expansion of the war in Vietnam, Cambodia, and Laos.

Q

is for QANON. A far-far-right, conspiracy theory that believes the country is controlled by a satanic, cannibal, pedophiles running a global child sex-trafficking ring who worked against former U.S. president Donald Trump while he was in office.

R

is for ROD BLAGOJEVICH. In 2008, this Illinois Governor tried to sell Barack Obama's former U.S. Senate seat to the highest bidder. Removed from office for abuse of power and corruption, he was indicted by a federal grand jury and found guilty on all charges pertaining to the Senate seat, and extortion. Blagojevich went to prison in 2012 but was pardoned by President Donald Trump in 2020.

S is for **STATE CAPTURE**. This is when non-governmental, outside interests, are able to manipulate laws, regulations and policies for their financial gain. A global example would be drug lords in Mexico that control the country through corrupt dealings with politicians and public officials. In the U.S., State capture is done more so by corporations using their tremendous wealth to dictate laws and policies to their own benefit using weak, cowardly politicians.

T is for Ted Kennedy. Chappaquiddick, 1969, Ted was leaving a party with 28-year-old passenger Mary Jo Kopechne, and drove his car off a bridge into the water. He swam away but Mary Jo was trapped inside the vehicle. A diver recovered Mary Jo's body around 9am the following morning - an hour before Ted reported what had happened from the previous night. He was sentenced to two months, suspended.

UNSCRUPULOUS. This is when a politician is dishonest, immoral, unethical and has no conscious about the crimes they commit and the damage they do to the people who voted for them and our country. Oddly, this is also the same definition of "politician" today. Beyond having no respect for basic principles of right and wrong, they are contemptuous of what is honorable, just, and true. Other words for unscrupulous include unprincipled, weasel, dirt bag, senator, and representative.

V is for **VOTER FRAUD.** This is when there's illegal interference with the process of an election. This could include impersonation at the polls, false registrations, duplicate voting, fraudulent use of absentee ballots, buying votes, illegal "assistance" at the polls, ineligible voting, altering the vote count, and ballot petition fraud. The history of U.S. elections has numerous examples of this.

W is for Watergate. This is the name of an office-apartment-hotel complex in Washington, D.C. where five men were arrested for breaking into the Democratic National Headquarters. Many senior officials in President Richard Nixon's administration were convicted. Nixon was impeached for obstruction of justice, abuse of power, and contempt of Congress but resigned from office on August 9, 1974 before he could be tried. He remains the only President to have resigned from office. Nixon was later given a full pardon by President Gerald Ford, his former Vice President.

Y

is for YELLOW DOG DEMOCRAT. This was a voter from the South that swore that they would "vote for a yellow dog" before they'd vote for a Republican. It is important to note that the Democratic party was the pro-slavery party and maintained control of the South well into the 20th century including blocking passage of anti-lynching legislation in the 1930s and 1940s.

X

is for XENOCRACY. Traditionally it's when a country is ruled by foreigners or foreign forces. An example of this would be when India was ruled by the British. Today the United States is a xenocracy because it's ruled by U.S. and foreign corporations, banks, and dark money.

Z

is for ZOO PLANE. The aircraft that accompanies Air Force One that carries the media equipment, technicians, and press pool that is out of favor with the administration. Passengers on this plane are referred to as animals.

Democracy is a wonderful thing - a "government of the people, by the people, for the people…" allows for all the citizens to have their voices heard in shaping a nation for everyone. Unfortunately, this is not the case in today's America (maybe it never was). We are a government of corporations and the ultra-wealthy, by corporations and the ultra-wealthy, for corporations and the ultra-wealthy.

The system is corrupt, and broken, and those in power, especially the career politicians, know it and work very hard to keep it that way. To them, money and power will always come before the working-class and the poor. Both parties, red and blue, are equally dirty and equally owned.

Citizens United vs. FEC. The Supreme Court, in a 5-4 decision, sold the soul of our nation and legalized the complete corruption of our political system. Congress can take action to change this but they haven't because it legitimizes their corruption.

"I think the notion that we have all the democracy that money can buy strays so far from what our democracy is supposed to be. I think members of the legislature, people who have to run for office, know the connection between money and influence on what laws get passed."

- Supreme Court Justice Ruth Bader Ginsburg speaking on why Citizens United was the court's worst decision ever.

There isn't a single issue we face today that cannot be fixed, but not until the political system is restored to true democracy will this happen (peacefully).

A corrupt system cannot, and will not, fix itself. There is just too much money on the table in politics to do the right thing. We'll hear their reform rhetoric, playing to the cameras and the internet, but it's just that – rhetoric, a verbal sleight of hand, to fool us while keeping the status quo corruption intact. Their contempt for us bleeds into every aspect of our lives and the future of our nation.

29

Made in the USA
Middletown, DE
23 June 2021